Start the Code

Student Workbook

William Collins' dream of knowledge for all began with the publication of his first book in 1819.
A self-educated mill worker, he not only enriched millions of lives, but also founded a flourishing publishing house.
Today, staying true to this spirit, Collins books are packed with inspiration, innovation and practical expertise.
They place you at the centre of a world of possibility and give you exactly what you need to explore it.

Published by Collins
An imprint of HarperCollins*Publishers*
The News Building, 1 London Bridge Street, London, SE1 9GF, UK

HarperCollins*Publishers*
Macken House, 39/40 Mayor Street Upper, Dublin 1, D01 C9W8, Ireland

Browse the complete Collins catalogue at
collins.co.uk

© Wandle Learning Trust 2026
littlewandlecode.org.uk

10 9 8 7 6 5 4 3 2 1

A catalogue record for this publication is available from the British Library.

ISBN 978-0-00-879102-5

All rights reserved. No part of this publication may be reproduced, stored in a retrieval system, or transmitted in
any form by any means, electronic, mechanical, photocopying, recording or otherwise, without the prior written
permission of the Publisher or a licence permitting restricted copying in the United Kingdom issued by the
Copyright Licensing Agency Ltd, 5th Floor, Shackleton House, 4 Battle Bridge Lane, London SE1 2HX.

Without limiting the exclusive rights of any author, contributor or the publisher of this publication, any unauthorised use
of this publication to train generative artificial intelligence (AI) technologies is expressly prohibited. HarperCollins also
exercise their rights under Article 4(3) of the Digital Single Market Directive 2019/790 and expressly reserve this publication
from the text and data mining exception.

Little Wandle Code has been developed by
Wandle Learning Trust in collaboration with Collins.

At Wandle Learning Trust:
Author: Sarah Paxton
Project manager: Rachel Russ
Editors: Helen Lawson, Caroline Hale, Tracy Kewley
Proofreaders: Jane Jackson, Jennie Clifford
Cover designer: Communitas
Internal designers and typesetters: Communitas, Tech-Set

At Collins:
Publisher: Katie Sergeant
Product manager: Natasha Paul
Production controller: Sophie Waeland

Printed in the UK

Acknowledgements

The publishers gratefully acknowledge the permission
granted to reproduce the copyright material in this book.
Every effort has been made to trace copyright holders
and to obtain their permission for the use of copyright
material. The publishers will gladly receive any information
enabling them to rectify any error or omission at the first
opportunity.

Mnemonic illustrations by Noah Warnes
Other illustrations by Marek Jagucki, apart from
p. 7: New Vectors/Shutterstock

Contents

Unit 1 (Sessions 1.1 to 1.4)	5
Unit 2 (Sessions 2.1 to 2.3)	9
Unit 3 (Sessions 3.1 to 3.3)	15
Unit 4 (Sessions 4.1 to 4.4)	21
Unit 5 (Sessions 5.1 to 5.4)	27
Unit 6 (Sessions 6.1 to 6.4)	33
Unit 7 (Sessions 7.1 to 7.4)	39
Unit 8 (Sessions 8.1 to 8.4)	45
Unit 9 (Sessions 9.1 to 9.4)	51
Start the Code Chart	62
Glossary	64

Session 1.1
Table 1

	👉	✏️
sun	3	sun
cat		
dog		
man		
sock		
ship		

Session 1.3

Tricky Words Grid

2.1, 2.2	the	I	no	go
3.1, 3.2	to	of	he	she
4.1, 4.2	we	me	be	was
5.1, 5.2	you	they	my	are
6.1, 6.2	all	her	said	so
7.1, 7.2	have	like	some	come
8.1, 8.2	love	do	were	here
9.1, 9.2	when	what	one	out

Session 1.4
You as a Reader

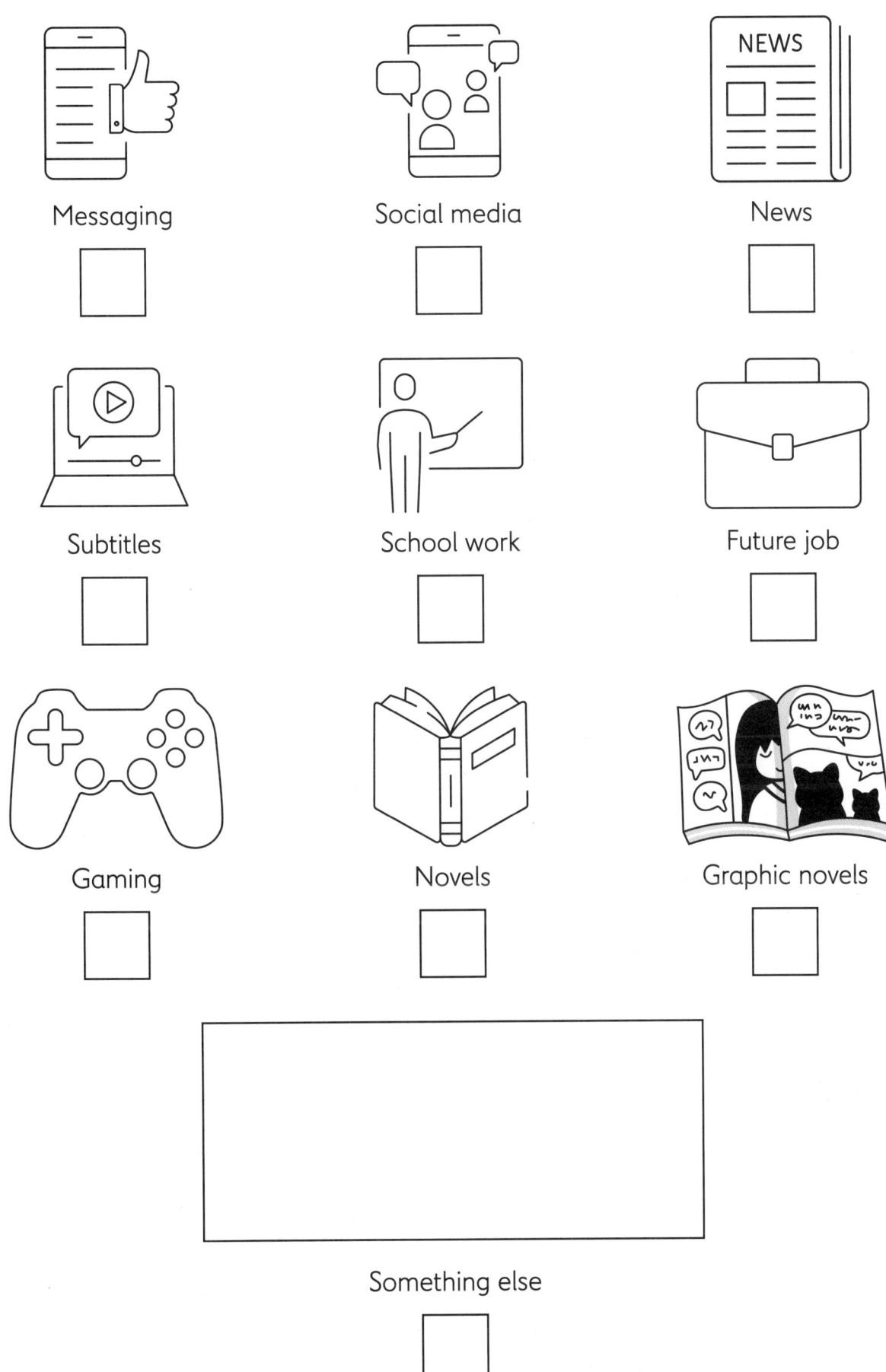

Code Agreement

I agree to:

- Follow instructions

- Listen to my teacher

- Be kind to my peers

- Not give up, even when it is hard

- Remember that mistakes help me learn

- Ask for help if I need it

- Take my reading learning seriously.

Signed _____

Session 2.1 s, a, t, p, i, n

Learn New Code

s   s   s

a   a   a

t   t   t

p   p   p

i   i   i

n   n   n

Learn Curriculum Words

1. _____

2. _____

3. _____

4. _____

Summary

s, a, t, p, i, n		
tap	pan	sip
snip	sat	sit
pit	pat	
span		

Session 2.2 s, a, t, p, i, n

Map it

t	n	a
s	p	i

Learn New Code

s　s　s

a　a　a

t　t　t

p　p　p

i　i　i

n　n　n

Learn Curriculum Words

1. _____
2. _____
3. _____
4. _____

Summary

s, a, t, p, i, n		
pin	spin	snip
ant	pants	pip
at	sat	snips
sit	sip	tin
tip	tap	
sap	snap	

Session 2.3

Write it

s   s   s

a   a   a

t   t   t

p   p   p

i   i   i

n   n   n

Make it

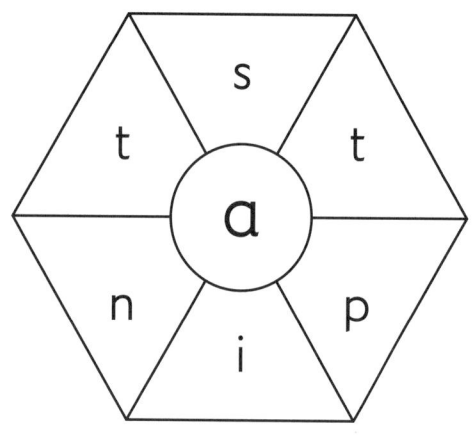 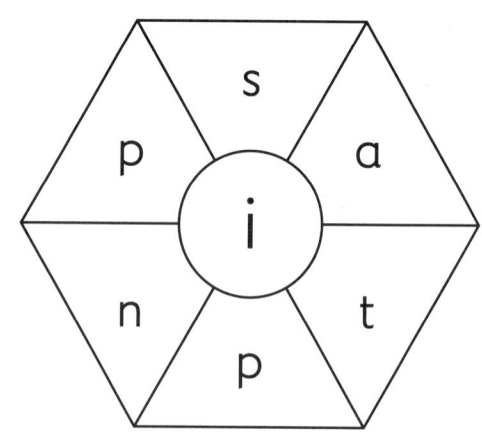

Session 3.1 m, d

Map it

a	s	p
i	t	n

Learn New Code

m   m   m

d   d   d

Learn Curriculum Words

1. _____

2. _____

3. _____

4. _____

Summary

m, d		Review	
man	dips	sat	pat
spam	sand	spat	spit
dim	dad	spin	span
sad	stand	pan	pant
did		pants	ants

Session 3.2 m, d

Map it

a	m	t	d
p	s	n	i

Learn New Code

m   m.   m.

d   d.   d.

Learn Curriculum Words

1. _____

2. _____

3. _____

4. _____

Summary

m, d		Review	
mint	stand	spit	pit
stamp	panda	sit	sip
map	man	snip	snap
spam	and	pan	
sand	sandpit		

Session 3.3

Write it

m   m   m

d   d   d

s   s   s

a   a   a

t   t   t

p   p   p

Make it

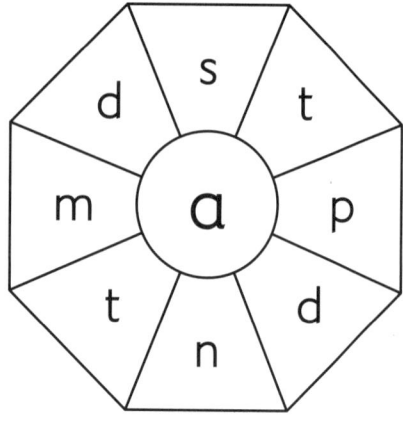
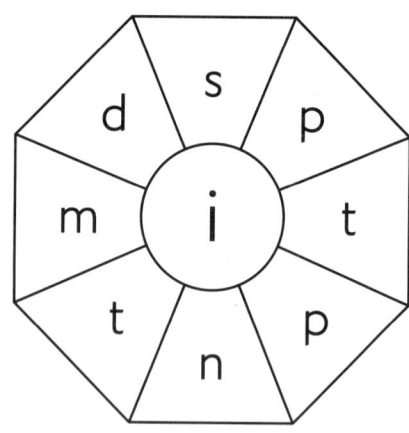

Session 4.1 g, o, c

Map it

d	i	s	t
p	a	n	m

Learn New Code

g g g

o o o

c c c

Learn Curriculum Words

1. _____

2. _____

3. _____

4. _____

Summary

g, o, c		Review	
act	magma	map	dam
gas	comic	damp	stand
gap	cap	stamp	and
camp	stomp	sand	span
		an	panda
		pan	

Session 4.2 k, ck

Map it

m	c	a	o	g
d	t	i	n	p

Learn New Code

k k k

ck ck ck

Learn Curriculum Words

1. _____

2. _____

3. _____

4. _____

Summary

k, ck		Review	
attack	mask	sip	map
stick	skip	cap	gap
sick	sack	gas	cast
stack	stock	cost	cosmic
		comic	panic
		picnic	impact

Session 4.4

Write it

g g g

o o o

c c c

k k k

ck ck ck

m m m

Make it

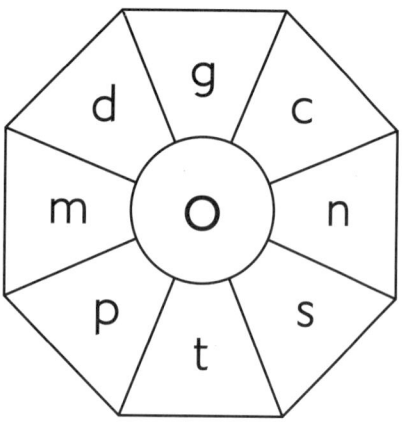 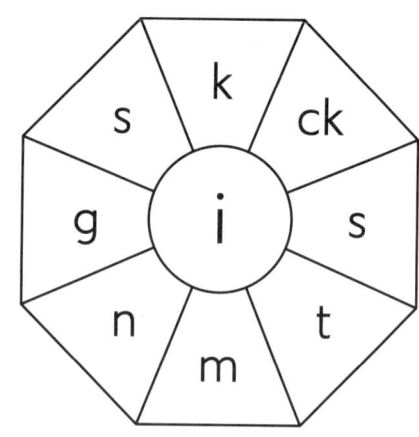

Session 5.1 e, u

Map it

g	i	o	t
c	a	m	d
k	n	ck	s

Learn New Code

e   e   e

u   u   u

Learn Curriculum Words

1. _____

2. _____

3. _____

4. _____

Summary

e, u		Review	
magnet	tectonic	smack	stack
sunset	summit	sack	sock
socket	pocket	sick	stick
packet	unpack	tick	pick
		pack	pad

Session 5.2 r, h

Map it

d	k	g	e
ck	o	u	m
c	p	a	t

Learn New Code

r r r

h h h

Learn Curriculum Words

1. _____

2. _____

3. _____

4. _____

Summary

r, h		Review	
present	rocket	deck	duck
attract	hack	tuck	stuck
crust	rust	muck	peck
rest	rent	pick	pen
		pest	test
		tent	content

Session 5.4

Write it

e   e   e

u   u   u

r   r   r

h   h   h

g   g   g

o   o   o

Make it

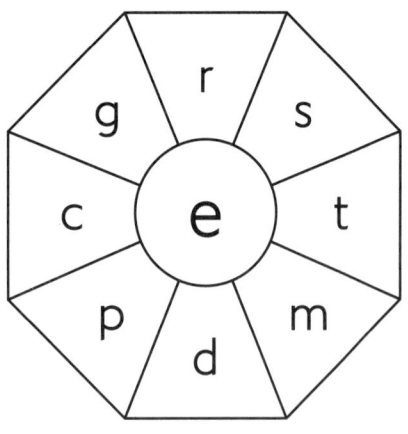

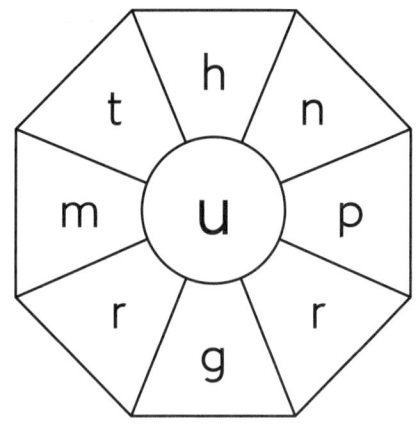

Session 6.1 b, l, ll

Map it

e	g	c	u
h	r	k	o
m	ck	d	s

Learn New Code

b b b

l l l

Learn Curriculum Words

1. _____

2. _____

3. _____

4. _____

Summary

b, l, ll		Review	
parallel	habitat	hint	hunt
laptop	pollen	hand	handstand
back	black	stand	stamp
bland	blend	strap	scrap
bend	bell	ramp	cramp

Session 6.2 f, ff, ss, j

Map it

u	b	g	r
e	ck	h	l
o	ll	m	d

Learn New Code

Learn Curriculum Words

1. _____

2. _____

3. _____

4. _____

Summary

f, ff, ss, j		Review	
traffic	blossom	end	bend
inject	fabric	send	sell
cliff	sniff	bell	belt
affect	staff	bent	best
infect		bust	bump

Session 6.4

Write it

Make it

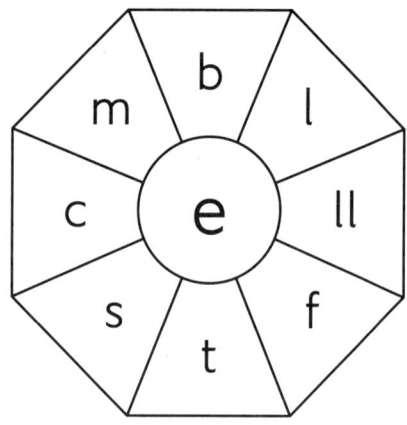
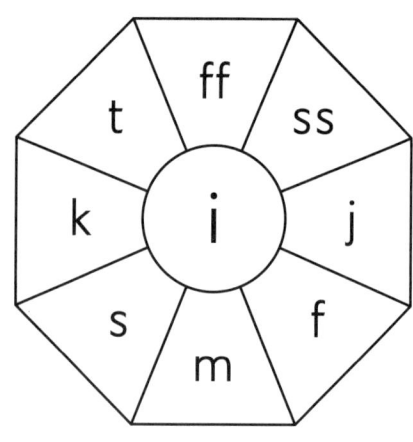

Session 7.1 v, w, y

Map it

l	h	f	r
ff	s	j	ss
b	u	ll	e

Learn New Code

v   v   v

w   w   w

y   y   y

Learn Curriculum Words

1. _____

2. _____

3. _____

4. _____

Summary

v, w, y		Review	
cobweb	windmill	just	jump
festival	yell	lump	stump
well	wet	stuff	fluff
west	vest	floss	loss
vet	velvet	less	stress

Session 7.2 x, z, zz

Map it

o	f	d	w
ff	v	j	ss
b	l	ll	y

Learn New Code

X x x

Z z z

Learn Curriculum Words

1. _____
2. _____
3. _____
4. _____

Summary

x, z, zz		Review	
Brazil	fizz	west	vest
index	suffix	vet	yet
buzz	fuzz	yell	well
fix	fox	will	win
box		wind	windmill

Session 7.4

Write it

v   v   v

w   w   w

y   y   y

x   x   x

z   z   z

b   b   b

Make it

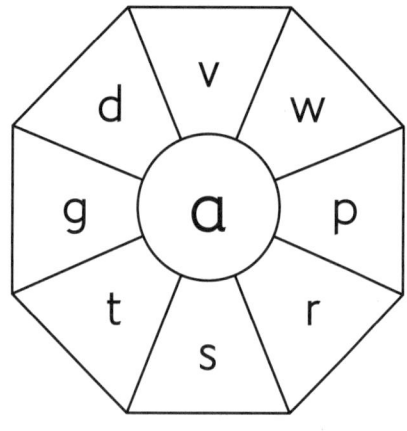 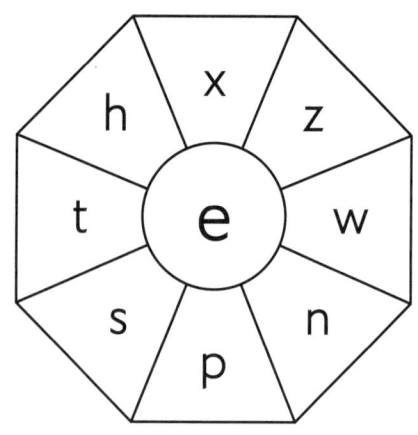

Session 8.1 qu

Map it

h	j	f	x
r	zz	v	y
b	z	w	ll

Learn New Code

qu qu qu

Learn Curriculum Words

1. _____

2. _____

3. _____

4. _____

Summary

qu		Review	
squid	liquid	vest	zest
quick	quicksand	best	bust
quit	quiz	buzz	fuzz
quid		fizz	fix
		fox	box

Session 8.2 ch, sh

Map it

u	h	z	e
ss	l	b	ll
x	r	zz	qu

Learn New Code

ch ch ch

sh sh sh

Learn Curriculum Words

1. _____

2. _____

3. _____

4. _____

Summary

ch, sh		Review	
rubbish	attach	quack	quick
children	astonish	quiz	quizzes
crunch	hunch	quit	quilt
bunch	bench	quill	quid
French	fresh	squid	liquid

Session 8.4

Write it

qu qu qu

ch ch ch

sh sh sh

v v v

y y y

j j j

Make it

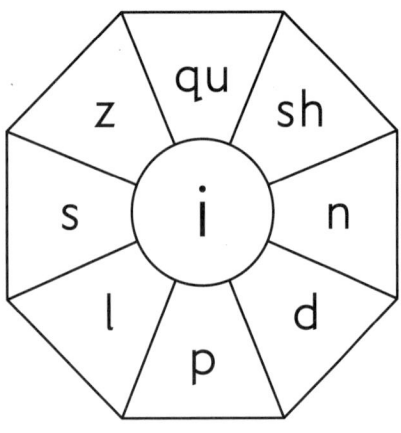 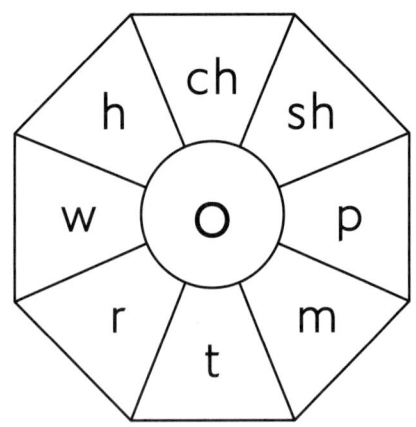

Session 9.1 th

Map it

x	j	v	zz
qu	w	ch	z
sh	f	y	ff

Learn New Code

th th th

Learn Curriculum Words

1. _____

2. _____

3. _____

4. _____

Summary

th		Review	
marathon	mammoth	ship	shop
sloth	maths	shock	mock
thump	thick	muck	much
thin		munch	lunch
		crunch	scrunch
		stump	stuck
		stick	

Session 9.2 ng, nk

Map it

f	e	th	b
qu	ch	u	sh
s	r	ss	h

Learn New Code

ng ng ng

nk nk nk

Learn Curriculum Words

1. _____

2. _____

3. _____

4. _____

Summary

ng, nk		Review	
bankrupt	spring	broth	froth
shrink	strong	cloth	sloth
bring	string	moth	goth
thing	think	gothic	thick
thinking		thin	then

Session 9.4

Write it

th   th   th

ng   ng   ng

nk   nk   nk

ch   ch   ch

u   u   u

e   e   e

Make it

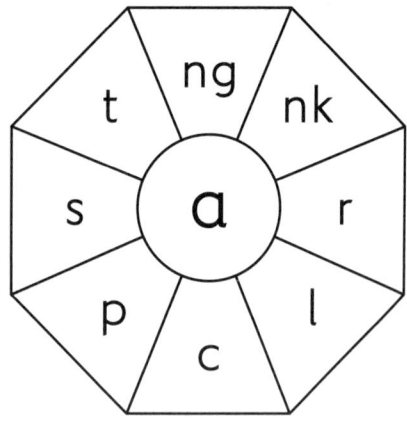
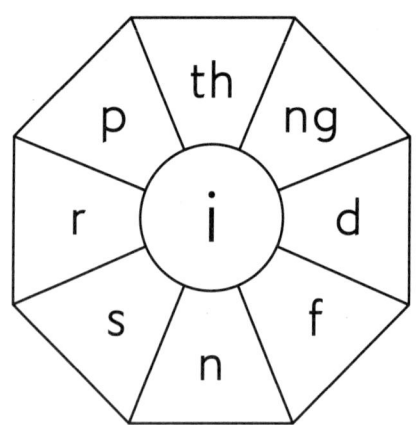

Start the Code Chart

Consonants

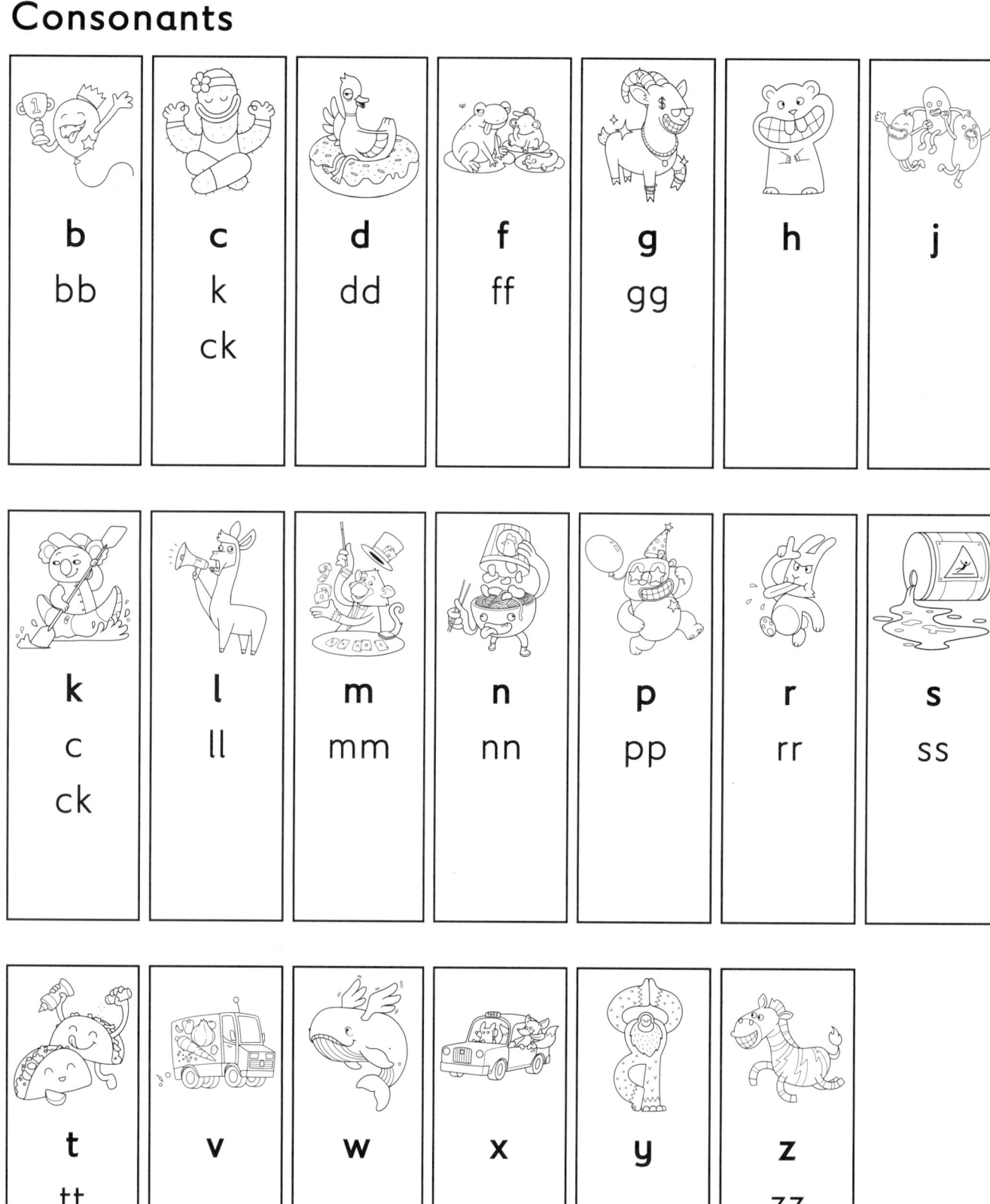

Consonant Digraphs

Vowels

Glossary

blend: We blend phonemes together to make a word. For example, c-a-t is blended together to make the word 'cat'.

code it out loud: When we code a word out loud, we say each of the phonemes in the word. For example, the word 'cat' coded out is c-a-t.

digraph: Two letters that together make one phoneme (sound). For example, the digraph 'sh' makes the sound /sh/ in the word 'shot'.

grapheme: A letter, or group of letters, that represents a phoneme (sound). For example, the word 'cat' has three graphemes: 'c', 'a' and 't'.

phoneme: A sound within a word. For example, there are three phonemes in the word 'cat': /c/, /a/, /t/.

schwa: An unstressed vowel sound that is in a lot of words. It sounds a bit like 'uh'. For example, in the word 'doctor', the second vowel sound is a schwa. In 'elephant', the final vowel sound is a schwa.

syllable: A beat of sound within a word. For example, the word 'sunset' has two syllables: 'sun' and 'set'.

tricky word: A common word that cannot be decoded easily because it contains one or more unusual graphemes. For example, in the word 'of', the grapheme 'f' makes the sound /v/.

tweak it: When we tweak it, we slightly adjust how we say a word to make it sound right. For example, for 'doctor', we say 'doct-UH' not 'doct-OR'.